THE JEWISH CHILDREN'S BIBLE

GENESIS

Adapted by Sheryl Prenzlau

PITSPOPANY

NEW YORK ◆ JERUSALEM

Jacob marries Rachel.

Text copyright ©1996 by Sheryl Prenzlau
Illustrations copyright © 1996 by Zely Smekhov, Daniel Goldberg, Lena Guberman

Design: Benjie Herskowitz

Published by Pitspopany Press
Pitspopany Press books may be purchased for educational or special sales use.
For information, please write:
Marketing Director, Pitspopany Press, 555 Chestnut Street, Cedarhurst, New York 11516.
Or fax: 212 472-6253.

ISBN: 0-943706-31-9

Printed in Israel

Contents

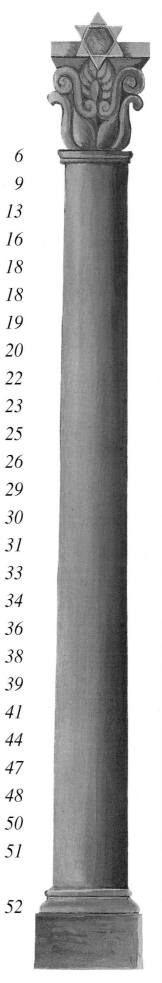

Foreword

Publishing a Jewish children's Bible, is not a simple task, on any level. Choosing the stories that will most appeal to young children; adapting these stories so the reader will get the most out of them; utilizing rabbinic material that will help clarify difficult passages and events, without changing the stories themselves; and integrating each story with illustrations that are both visually pleasing and that fill-in where words seem inadequate, make publishing a children's Bible different from any other children's book.

That's why we have divided GENESIS into two distinct parts. The first section presents the stories of many of the major events in the Bible on a level children, with the help of their parents and teachers, can appreciate. We have been very careful not to be didactic; but, rather, we encourage parents to present the Jewish values they see in these stories, to their children.

Some Bible books for children do not illustrate the faces of the forefathers. We have consciously decided to portray all the Bible characters in vivid color because trying to hide the faces of the characters would have been too contrived. For example, showing the meeting of Jacob with his son, Joseph, after many decades of separation, would have been impossible if the emotions on their faces had to be hidden. More importantly, we felt that the storyline, when reenforced by quality illustrations, would greatly enhance the child's appreciation of the Torah. Naturally, a parent or teacher can tell the child that these pictures are just the illustrator's representation of what our forefathers looked like. When it comes to the Torah, you cannot be *parve*; the stories are so filled with meaning, morality, innuendo, it is hard to just re-write them. Indeed, without the use of a commentary at certain crucial times it would be difficult for adults, let alone children, to understand what was happening. Therefore, whenever the fact pattern was unclear, the author, Sheryl Prenzlau, incorporated the suggestions of the master commentator, *Rashi*, who so successfully made the Torah accessible to generations of Jews.

A case in point is the battle of Jacob with the angel. As it stands, it is unclear why the angel fought with him, or even if he was an angel. So, Mrs. Prenzlau uses Rashi's explanation of the incident, which answers this and other such questions, for young and old alike.

The second section of GENESIS presents *Midrashim*, rabbinic interpretations and behind-the-scenes accounts of many of the Biblical stories. The Midrashim should be used by parents and teachers to further enhance the

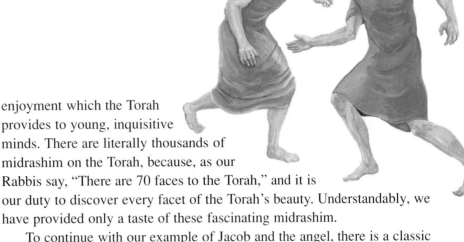

enjoyment which the Torah provides to young, inquisitive minds. There are literally thousands of midrashim on the Torah, because, as our Rabbis say, "There are 70 faces to the Torah," and it is our duty to discover every facet of the Torah's beauty. Understandably, we have provided only a taste of these fascinating midrashim.

To continue with our example of Jacob and the angel, there is a classic question many children and adults ask about this story: Why is it that just because Jacob limped after being wounded in his thigh by the angel, Jews are forbidden from eating the *Gid Ha'Nasheh*, the similar sinew found in the thigh of kosher animals? By referring to our Midrashim section, the reader will discover at least one of the rabbinic explanations for this law.

As for the illustrations, we have chosen to meld the pictures into the body of the story, so that picture and story become one. In order to achieve the maximum visual affect for each story, we worked with a team of illustrators, oftentimes deciding from a group of similar illustrations which one best expressed a particular event or scene.

Producing GENESIS, and the other four volumes of THE JEWISH CHILDREN'S BIBLE is truly a labor of the heart, and it is only fitting that our dedicated staff should get recognition:

A hearty *ya'asher kochacha* (congratulations) to Chaim Mazo for making sure the production aspect of this book would be as perfect as possible.

Dorothy Tananbaum worked tirelessly, as she always does, to market this series to the general trade and the chain stores. In this way we are able to reach those Jews who opt not to visit their local Jewish bookstore or don't have a Jewish bookstore in their locality.

Others who have been extremely helpful in this project include: Rabbi Macy Gordon and Rabbi Sholom Gold, who reviewed the manuscript. Carmi Schwartz, our liaison to the Jewish community organizations. Malcolm Hoenlein who, as executive vice chairman of The Conference of Presidents of Major Jewish Organizations, enthusiastically supported our project. Charlotte Frank, who has been a constant guiding light to us and has helped us navigate the general market waters.

Some people have an everlasting affect on you. Such a person was my mentor, Rabbi Shlomo Freifeld, of blessed memory. His love for Jews — all Jews — was an inspiration to me, and serves as a guiding light of our company.

Rabbi Yaacov Peterseil, Publisher
PITSPOPANY PRESS
Jerusalem, Israel

In The Beginning...

Before God created the world —
Before there were people or animals or plants
or water —
There was nothing. Nothing at all.
There was only God.
And God said:
LET THERE BE LIGHT!
And in a flash, there was light.
God saw that the light was good, and God split

בראשית...

the light into Day and Night.
That was what happened on Day One.
God then made fire and water, mixed
them together, and made the heavens above
and the waters below.
That was what happened on the Second Day.
Then God put all the waters
together, and made the seas.

God called the
dry land, Earth.
And God said:
*Let Grass And Herbs And Trees
Come Out Of The Earth.*
And when God saw the grass and herbs
and trees, God saw that it was good.
That was what happened on the Third Day.
Next, God put the sun and the moon into the heavens, and
the stars there to help the moon light up the night.
That's how we can count days, months, and even seasons
and years.
And God saw that it was good.
That was what happened on the Fourth Day.
God filled the seas with fish of all sizes and the sky with all
kinds of birds and flying creatures, like mosquitos, and bees,
and butterflies. And God made all sorts of bugs and tiny
creeping things crawl along the earth.
God blessed the fish and the birds and the flying
creatures, and even the creepy crawlers, and told them
all to have many children.
And God saw that it was good.
That was what happened on the Fifth Day.

But God wasn't finished yet. God then created all the animals – the wild ones, like lions and tigers and bears, and the tame ones, like cows and goats and sheep.

And God saw that it was good.

But something was missing.

Man.

So God took dust from the four corners of the earth.

Then, God mixed the dust with some water, and formed it into a man.

Then, God said:

I Will Call This Man, Adam, Because He Comes From The Adama, The Ground.

God breathed into Adam's nose, and gave him a soul, so that he could think and speak. Then he took a rib from Adam's chest and created Woman.

And God blessed Adam and his wife and said:

You Will Rule Over All The Animals, Fish, Birds, And Every Creeping Thing.

And God saw that this was very good.

That was what happened on the Sixth Day.

Then God completed everything that was created in the heavens and the earth.

This was a very special day, the Seventh Day, the Shabbat.

And God blessed the Shabbat, and it became a day of rest for all the world to enjoy.

The Garden Of Eden

God took Adam and his wife and put them into *Gan Eden*, the Garden of Eden.

Then God said to Adam: "You can eat anything you want in this garden, except for the fruit of The Tree of Knowledge, the *Aytz Ha'daat*."

Then God brought all the living things to Adam and asked him to give them names. Adam also gave his wife a name. He called her *Eshah*, which means Woman. Later, he also called her *Chavah*, which means Life-Giver, because she gave life to their children. Today, many people use her English name, Eve.

The Garden of Eden was filled with every type of sweet-smelling plant and tree you could imagine. Eve loved to stroll in the garden, tasting different fruits that grew there. She was munching on a particularly delicious fruit when suddenly she saw a tall thin creature, watching her.

"I am called Snake," the creature hissed, "and I was just wondering about something, Woman."

Eve looked at the skinny snake, who was crawling down a nearby tree on little salamander legs..

"How can I help you?" the woman asked him.

"Is it true you can eat *all* the fruits in the garden, except one?" the snake asked her.

"Yes," Eve answered, not knowing how tricky the snake could be. "Adam told me that God said we could eat from all of the fruits in the garden except for the fruits from the Tree of Knowledge. See it right there?" she said, walking towards the tree. "God said we can't even touch it!"

But that wasn't really true. Eve added that part herself.

"Oh, is that so," said the snake, with a sly smile. Suddenly he ran over to her and pushed her into the Tree of Knowledge. Eve let out a cry.

"Look, Woman," the snake hissed. "You touched the tree and nothing happened. Believe me, if you *eat* from the tree, nothing will happen to you either."

The woman thought about that, but she wasn't sure. Then the tricky snake said, "Do you know why God doesn't want you to eat from this tree?"

The woman looked at the snake and shook her head.

"It's because God ate from this tree, and that's why God's so smart, smart enough to make the whole world. If you eat from the tree you will become just as smart as God."

The woman thought some more. No one had ever lied to her before, so she trusted her new "friend", the snake. She liked the Garden of Eden, but she would also have liked to make her own world, just like God did.

So she reached out, pulled off a mouth-watering fruit and took a big bite. Nothing bad happened. So she ran to Adam and convinced him to take a bite too.

But then Adam and Eve started feeling strange. They looked at each other and realized they had done something wrong. God had said not to eat from the Tree of Knowledge, and they had not listened. That was bad. Very bad.

What will happen when God finds out? Adam and Eve wondered. Then they heard a strange noise.

It was God!

"I think we'd better hide," Adam said. And they ran into the bushes and crouched very low.

"Where are you?" God called out to Adam.

At first Adam thought that if they were real quiet maybe God wouldn't find them. But then he realized that God knows everything and only wanted Adam to be brave and admit to what he had done.

"I'm sorry, God," Adam spoke up, in a scared voice. "I was embarrassed."

"Embarrassed? About what?" God asked, waiting for Adam to tell the truth. When Adam didn't answer right away, God said, "Did you do something you weren't supposed to do? Did you eat

from the Tree of Knowledge, after I told you not to?"

"Yes, God," Adam admitted quietly. "But I did it because the Woman you gave me brought me the fruit to eat. *She* convinced me to taste it," he said, pointing to Eve.

"What have you done?" God asked the frightened Eve.

"It was the *snake* who tricked me into eating the fruit," she argued, pointing to the snake.

The snake wasn't even embarrassed. He lifted himself as high as his legs could carry him, looking almost proud of what he had done.

"Because you did this," God told the snake, "I am taking away your legs. You will crawl forever on your belly and eat dust. People will never trust you. They will always hate you and will want to crush you!

"As for you, Eve," God declared, "you will have to depend on your husband for many things. Also, giving birth to children will be very uncomfortable for you, from now on."

"And Adam," God continued, "this was supposed to be your garden to enjoy forever. But now, you will have to work very hard to make the ground give you food."

Yet God still loved Adam and Eve. He made them special clothing so they would be warm and dry. Because God had decided that they couldn't live in Gan Eden anymore, God took them out of the garden, and placed special angels with swords of fire to stand at the gates of the garden and guard it from man, forever.

Noah And The Flood   נח

Adam and Eve had many children. As time went by, their descendents became selfish and spiteful. They stole from each other and lied to each other, and did even worse things than that.

Only one man loved God: Noah.

God decided that if so many people were going to act mean and terrible, then it was time to destroy the world. Only Noah, his wife, and their three sons, Shem, Cham, and Yafet, would be permitted to live.

One day, God spoke to Noah.

"Noah," God said. "The people are very wicked. So I have decided to destroy them. Only you and your family will remain in My world.

"I want you to build a special boat, called an Ark, and cover it on the inside and on the outside with tar, so water can't come in. Build the Ark three stories high, with room for lots of animals, and for all of your family. I will bring you two of every animal, and seven pairs of the animals you may eat."

Noah began building the Ark exactly the way God had told him to. But the wicked people around him made fun of him whenever they could.

"What a silly man!" said one fellow.

"Yes," another agreed. "What good is a boat when we are not near an ocean, or even a lake?"

But Noah ignored their teasing. He just continued building the Ark.

In those days, people lived a long time. And when Noah was 600 years old, he finished building the Ark. Noah's family helped him carry in enough food for all of them and for many, many animals.

As Noah stood at the entrance to the Ark, he looked up at the long line of animals forming in front of him. Just as God had told him, there were two of every animal and bird, even of the little creeping creatures, and seven pairs of those animals he would one day be permitted to eat.

"Stay in line," Noah told the animals. "There will be room for all of you."

Noah stood and watched until all of the animals were inside. Then, as it started to drizzle, Noah went inside. The drizzle turned into a downpour and the downpour, turned into a torrent, and the torrent turned into a flood!

By then, the people outside realized that Noah had been right! But it was too late. The rains came down harder and harder, until the Ark began to float.

For forty days and nights, the rain came down without stopping. The water rose higher and higher, until even the mountains were covered! Noah and his family kept busy feeding the animals and cleaning their cages.

When the rain finally stopped, Noah opened up the window on

the Ark. All he saw for miles and miles was water. Finally, the water started going down, until the Ark rested on the very top of a mountain called Mt. Ararat.

Noah wanted to find out how much the waters had gone down. He called a raven and said, "Go out, bird, go out and find land."

The raven flew out, but soon came back. There was no land.

Noah waited a few more days and tried again. This time he sent a dove. But, again, the bird came back.

Finally, a few days later, Noah tried again. This time, the little

bird came back with an olive branch in her mouth.

"Thank you little bird," Noah told the dove. "Now I know that there are trees above the water. Soon, we will be able to leave the Ark."

The next time Noah sent the little dove out, the bird didn't come back. She had found a dry place to make her new home.

"It is time for all of you to find new homes," God said to Noah. "Open up the door, and let everyone out."

When everyone had gone out of the Ark, Noah thanked God for saving him and his family.

Then God made a promise to Noah.

"Look up at the sky," God said, as a beautiful, shimmering rainbow brightened up the sky. "This rainbow is a special sign to you and all your children. When you see, it you will know that I have kept my promise never to destroy the world again."

Noah was happy, for he knew that God's promises were always for keeps.

The Tower Of Babel

When, once again, there were many people in the world, they decided to rebel against God.

"Why is God greater than we are?" they asked each other. "We are many, we are strong, we are powerful. Why shouldn't we rule over God?"

Now, in those days everyone spoke the same language — Hebrew — and lived in the same part of the world. They thought that, as one people, they could do anything, even reach the sky.

"Let's build a tall tower right up to the Heavens," someone suggested. "Once we reach the top, we can take over God's world and rule."

"Good idea," agreed the others. "We'll all work together to build the biggest tower this world has ever seen."

And so, they began to build.

Many people joined together and made bricks, piling them higher and higher so that if you stood at the bottom of the tower you couldn't even see its top! God was happy that the people were working together, but sad that they were wasting all their energies in trying to build a tower to Heaven.

"What a waste of time and effort," God said to the angels. "I will have to teach them a lesson — one that will prevent them from ever doing this again.

"I will make each person speak a different language from now on," God decided.

And in a blink, what God said, happened.

One of the workers on the tower turned to his friend and said, "Please hand me that brick over there."

But all his friend heard him say was, "Bding gristed lampo tigder."

"What are you babbling about?" said the second man.

But the first man heard him mumble, "Gbksk trlodo protko pipplapa goo!"

"Stop speaking like a baby. I asked you for that brick," he repeated. But his friend continued to babble and wouldn't give him the brick. Finally, frustrated, he took the brick and hit his friend with it.

Angry and annoyed — and in quite a bit of pain — his friend took a brick and hit him back.

Soon, this scene was repeated all through the tower and everyone was hitting and screaming at each other. They couldn't understand what the other one was saying.

One by one the people left the tower. How could they fight against God, if they couldn't even understand each other?! The people finally gave up their plan, and many moved to different parts of the world — which is exactly what God wanted.

Abram And Lot לֶךְ לְךָ

Abram loved God more than anyone else in his day. So when God told him to leave his country, Abram took his wife, Sarai, his nephew, Lot, and everything he owned and started walking. He didn't even ask, "Where should I go?"

God led Abram to the land of Canaan. It was a big country, with land enough for everyone. But Lot's shepherds were forever fighting with Abram's shepherds. Lot's shepherds only wanted whatever land Abram's shepherds used for grazing their sheep.

Finally, one day, Abram said to Lot, "Why should there be so much fighting? There is plenty of room here for both of us. Choose somewhere else to live, and don't worry, I will always be nearby to help you if you need me."

Lot looked around for a grassy place to live. He chose to move near the wicked city of Sodom.

God Makes A Promise To Hagar

Sarai, Abram's wife, was sad because she couldn't have children, but she wanted Abram to have children. So she found a second wife (in those days people had more than one wife) for her husband. Her name was Hagar.

When Hagar became pregnant, she started to tease Sarai, saying, "I'm better than you because I'm going to have a baby and you can't." Hagar was so mean and cruel to Sarai that finally Sarai chased her out of their home, and Hagar fled into the desert.

Hagar ran and ran, until she found a well. There, an angel of God appeared to her and said, "Hagar, return to Sarai, because inside your body is a son of Abram. This son will be a man of the desert, fighting and warring with everyone. He will have many

descendants and his name will be Ishmael."

Hagar knew that she had to obey the angel of God, so she returned to Sarai and had her baby. Abram called the baby, Ishmael.

God Makes A Promise To Abraham

When Abram was 99 years old, God spoke to him, saying, "You will receive a great reward for believing in Me."

"But I have no children from my wife, Sarai," Abram answered. "Will everything I own go to Ishmael?"

"No," God assured him. "Because Ishmael is your son, I will make him a great nation, and bless him. But I promise you, you will have a wonderful child from Sarai. His name will be Isaac.

"Look up at the stars," God continued. "From Isaac will come many descendents, as many as there are stars in the sky, and they

will multiply and cover the face of the
earth. And I will give them this whole
country to live in, as far as you can see.
"And, as a sign of my love for you and
Sarai, from now on your name will be
changed to Abraham, and your wife's
name will be changed to Sarah."

Then God told Abraham to circumcise
himself — to make a *Brit Milah* — and to
circumcise all the males in his house who were eight
days or older. From then on, all the *Hebrews,* which was what
Abraham and his descendents were called, were to circumcise
their boys. This would be a sign that they had a special
connection to God.

And Abraham did all that God commanded him.

Two Terrible Cities   וירא

After Abraham's Brit Milah, God made the sun shine very
brightly so that no guests would bother him while he was getting
well. But Abraham sat at the door of his tent waiting for
company, anyway. Finally, when God saw how badly Abraham
wanted guests, God sent three angels, dressed as men, to visit
him. Abraham was very happy when he saw them coming, and he
prepared food and drink for his company.

Each of the three angels had a special job to do:

One of the angels came just to heal Abraham.

The second angel told Sarah, "You will have a son next year at
this time." Sarah laughed when she heard this, thinking that at
ninety, she was too old to have a son.

The third angel asked Abraham, "Which way to the city of
Sodom?"

Now, Sodom and its sister city, Gomorrah, were the two
wickedest cities in the world. God had seen all the terrible things
the people did there and decided to destroy these cities.

When Abraham heard God's plans, he was upset.

"Maybe all of the people in these cities aren't so bad," he told God. "Will You save the cities if there are fifty good people living there?"

God said, "Yes."

"What if there are forty-five good people?" Abraham asked.

God said, "Even if there are forty-five good people."

"And forty?" Abraham asked again.

"Forty, also," God agreed.

"Please don't be upset, God," Abraham pleaded, "But what if there are thirty good people there? Will You save the cities then too?"

"Yes, I will," God answered.

"And for twenty?" Abraham asked meekly.

"Yes, for twenty," God again agreed.

"Does that mean if there are only ten good people You will save them too?" Abraham asked, hoping God was not getting angry with him.

"All right, Abraham," God told him, "but no less than ten."

But there weren't even ten good people in the cities, so the third angel was sent out to destroy these terrible people.

By then, Abraham's nephew, Lot, had moved into Sodom with his family.

Two of the angels that had visited Abraham came to Sodom and warned Lot to leave. "Quickly take your family and leave the city before it is too late," the angels advised Lot. "But warn everyone not to turn around to look at what will happen."

Lot wanted to take his money and jewels, but the angels forced him and his family to leave Sodom right away. The minute they left, rain and fire hurtled down from the sky. A giant mushroom cloud exploded over the city. Lot's wife was curious. She heard all the noise and commotion and wanted to see what was happening. As she began to turn her head, she caught a glimpse of all the destruction — and she turned into a pillar of salt!

Abraham Passes The Test

Just as God had promised, Sarah gave birth to a son, Isaac. When Isaac was eight days old, Abraham gave him a Brit Milah. Years later, God appeared to Abraham and said, "I want you to take your son, Isaac, whom I know you love very much, and give him to Me on the mountain I will show you."

As always, Abraham did what God told him to do. He woke up early the next morning, saddled his donkey, and took his son Isaac and two other servants with him. After three days of traveling, Abraham looked up and saw a mountain covered with clouds. He knew this was the place God had meant.

"Stay here with the donkey," Abraham told the two servants. "And I will take Isaac up to the mountain, and we will pray there to God."

Isaac and Abraham went up the mountain, together. Isaac carried the wood that would be needed for the sacrifice to God, and Abraham carried a knife.

"But father," Isaac asked, "where is the lamb for the sacrifice?"

"God will provide the sacrifice," Abraham answered him. Suddenly, Isaac understood what Abraham was telling him. He, Isaac, was to be the sacrifice. God was asking for him back.

Like his father, Isaac was ready to do whatever God said.

When they arrived at the place where the sacrifice was to take place, Isaac put down the wood, lay down on the branches, and watched as Abraham lifted the knife above his head.

Then Abraham heard an angel of God say, "Stop! I did not really want you to give Me back your son. I only wanted to test you to see if you were willing to do it."

Just then, Abraham heard a noise in the bushes, and saw a ram caught by its horns.

"I will bring this ram as a sacrifice to God," Abraham said.

Then God spoke to Abraham.

"Because you were ready to give Me back your only son, whom you love so much, I will bless your children, and make them as many as the stars in the heavens and the sand on the seashores."

And Abraham knew he had passed the hardest test of all, and he was happy.

The Perfect Wife For Isaac
חיי שרה

Sarah died, and Abraham mourned for her and laid her to rest in a cave he had bought from one of the local tribes that lived in Canaan. This cave became known as "M'arat Ha'Machpelah", the cave where all the forefathers would be buried.

Abraham soon realized that it was time to find a wife for his son, Isaac. But he certainly couldn't pick a wife from the young girls who lived in Canaan. They all worshipped idols.

So he sent for his servant Eliezer, and said, "Go to the land of my family, and bring back a wife for my son Isaac, from among my relatives."

Eliezer went to Aram with many camels and many presents to find a wife for Isaac. But how would he know whom to pick?

"God," Eliezer said, when he arrived in Aram, "I need a sign from You to know which girl is the right one for Isaac. I will go to the well. There, I will ask the girls for some water. The one that says, 'Here is some water, and water for your camels as well,' she is the one who is right for my master, Isaac."

Before Eliezer had even finished describing the sign he wanted from God, a young girl named Rebeccah came towards him with a water pitcher on her shoulder.

"Please, may I have a drink of water from your pitcher?" Eliezer asked the girl.

The girl drew some water for Eliezer and said, "Here is some water, and water for your camels as well."

Eliezer was amazed. Those were the exact words he had asked for, as a sign from God. Could this girl also be from Abraham's own family?

"Whose daughter are you?" he asked.

"I am the daughter of Betuel, and the granddaughter of Nachor. Come, stranger, we have room at our home for you and for your camels."

Nachor! Eliezer thought to himself. That's Abraham's brother! She's the one I'm looking for!

Eliezer gave Rebeccah a golden ring, and two golden bracelets that he had brought along from Abraham's house. And then he said a silent prayer, "Thank you God for leading me straight to Abraham's family."

Rebeccah ran to tell her mother what had happened to her at the well. Her brother, Lavan, was very interested in hearing how Eliezer had met Rebeccah.

"Please stay with us," he said, inviting Eliezer into their house. Lavan listened while Eliezer told the family how Abraham had sent him to them to find a wife for Isaac. He told them about his plan to find the right wife for Isaac. He asked them if they would let him bring Rebeccah back to Abraham's house, so that she could marry Isaac.

"Let's ask her," Rebeccah's brother and mother answered. And they called Rebeccah.

"Yes, I will go," she said, without hesitating.

The very next morning, Rebeccah left with Eliezer for the journey back to Abraham's house. Eliezer had found the perfect wife for Isaac.

Twins תולדות

Isaac's wife, Rebeccah, was going to have a baby. In fact, she was expecting twins! When they were born, they were very different from each other. The older one was reddish and very hairy. His parents named him Esav. The younger one was smaller, and when he was born, he was holding onto his brother's heel, so they named him Yaacov, which comes from the Hebrew word for "heel." Today, many people use his English name, Jacob.

The brothers were twins, but they didn't act at all alike. Jacob loved to learn from his parents, and was kind and gentle. Esav loved to hunt and party. But, even though Esav was wild, he still respected his father, and Isaac was very proud of him.

One day, Esav came home from hunting and he was very hungry. His brother Jacob was busy cooking a big pot of red bean soup.

"Hmm, that smells so good," Esav said, hungrily.

"I'll trade you the soup for something you have," Jacob said.

"What do I have that you could want?" Esav asked.

"Well, you are the firstborn, and therefore, when our father blesses us, you'll get the first blessings. I know you really don't care about those blessings, but I do. So, I want to trade the soup for your blessings." Jacob answered.

"Who needs blessings?" Esav answered. "I would rather have some soup now than some blessings in the future. And, anyway, blessings don't fill your stomach," he added scornfully.

"Deal," Jacob said.

"Deal," Esav echoed, as he poured himself a bowl of thick soup.

Jacob Takes The Blessings

When Isaac grew old, his eyesight began to fail, and he wanted to bless his children before he died.

"Please come here," he called to Esav. "Go into the fields and hunt for me, and bring me some of that delicious meat that I like. And when you are done, I want to bless you."

Rebeccah, Isaac's wife, was standing nearby and she heard them talking.

"Isaac thinks that Esav is a good man," she said to herself.

"He doesn't realize that Esav spends all his time worshipping idols and being wicked. Why, he even sold his right to get the blessings of the firstborn, to Jacob. Therefore, these blessings should really go to Jacob, who loves God."

Rebeccah had a plan. She prepared some meat herself, and she gave Jacob fur clothes to wear, and told him to bring the food to Isaac.

At first, Jacob didn't want to fool his father, but he knew that the blessings really belonged to him. So, he did as his mother told him, and brought the food to Isaac.

"I am here, father," Jacob said, as he approached Isaac with the food. "God helped me find an animal right away. Please, come eat."

Isaac sensed that something was wrong. Esav never talked about God, and his voice sounded so much...so much like Jacob's.

"Let me touch you, Esav," Isaac said, wanting to be sure it was his eldest son.

When Isaac felt the fur, he was sure it was the hairy hands of Esav. Even so, he couldn't help but wonder, and said under his breath, "The voice is the voice of Jacob, but the hands are the hands of Esav."

Isaac ate and drank. Then he blessed Jacob with a wonderful blessing, saying,

"May God give you an abundant harvest wherever you go, and may the peoples of the world — even your brothers — honor and respect you. And know that anyone who says a bad word about you will be cursed by God, and all those who bless you will be blessed."

Jacob thanked his father, and left.

A minute after Jacob came out of his father's tent, Esav came running in with a plate of meat for his father.

"I am back, father, with your food," Esav announced. "Come eat."

Isaac began to tremble. Who was this bringing him food? If this was Esav, then who was just here? In a flash, Isaac realized what had happened.

"Your brother, Jacob, has just left," Isaac told Esav. "I thought he was you and I gave him your blessings," he explained.

Now, Esav remembered how he had traded the blessings for some soup, and he was angry at himself for having sold the blessings. But most of all, he was furious with Jacob for what he had done.

"Don't you have any blessings left for me?" Esav pleaded.

Isaac blessed Esav too, saying,

"You will have good land, live by the sword, and serve your brother. And there will be times when you will break loose from him, and go off on your own."

"This is not the blessing I want," Esav said to himself. "I hate Jacob for taking the better blessing. Some day I will get him back for this!"

Rebeccah saw how angry Esav was, and she quickly called to Jacob.

"Esav will want to get back at you. Go and run to my brother Lavan, and stay there until Esav calms down," she advised him.

Isaac also called to Jacob, saying, "Go to Lavan's house, and find a wife there from our family. And rest assured, you will have all the things that God promised to my father Abraham. All of those blessings will be for your children."

Jacob's Ladder ויצא

Jacob was on his way to his Uncle Lavan's house. When the sun went down, Jacob put some stones under his head for a pillow, and lay down to sleep. As he slept, he began to dream.

In his dream, Jacob saw a ladder standing between Heaven and Earth. Jacob could see angels climbing up and down the ladder. Then Jacob heard the voice of God saying, "I am the God of your grandfather Abraham, and your father Isaac. All of this land will be for you and your children, who will be as many as the dust of the earth. And I promise to always protect you."

Then Jacob woke up. "This is a very holy place," he thought. "This is the Gate of Heaven."

And he called the place *Bet-El*, the House of God.

Lavan's Tricks

Jacob continued traveling. One day, he saw a well, which had a large rock covering it. The rock was so heavy, it took many shepherds to lift it off the well. Just then, Rachel, Lavan's daughter, came to the well to water her father's flock. When he found out who she was, Jacob was so happy to meet his cousin that he raced over and pushed the heavy rock off the well all by himself!

Rachel was also delighted to meet her relative, and took Jacob to Lavan, her father. When Lavan heard who had come to visit, he hugged Jacob. Lavan remembered the gifts that Eliezer had brought with him when he came to take his sister, Rebeccah, for Isaac. He wondered if Jacob had brought gold and presents with him.

But Jacob had nothing to give to Lavan. He had come to hide at his uncle's house.

"Let me stay and work for you," Jacob said.

"What do you want in exchange for your work?" Lavan asked Jacob.

"I will work for you for seven years, if you will let me marry your younger daughter, Rachel."

"Agreed," Lavan said.

But, when the seven years were up, Lavan tricked Jacob. He disguised his older daughter, Leah, to look like Rachel, and Jacob ended up marrying her instead of Rachel.

"Why did you trick me?" Jacob asked Lavan angrily.

"In our city, the oldest daughter always gets married first," Lavan told him. "But if you promise to work another seven years, you can marry Rachel." (In those days, people had more than one wife.)

Jacob knew that he had been tricked, but he wanted to marry Rachel. So he agreed to work for another seven years. After he married Rachel, he worked six more years in order to earn his own flocks of sheep. During this time, Rachel and Leah gave

Jacob their servants, Bilhah and Zilpah, as wives. And, as always, Lavan tried many times to trick Jacob and take away everything he had earned.

Jacob Fights The Angel וישלח

After twenty years in Lavan's house, Jacob began the journey home. When he had left his parents many years earlier, he had gone by himself. Now he was returning home with sheep, cows, camels, four wives, and twelve children!

On the way, messengers came to tell Jacob that Esav was coming with four hundred armed men!

Jacob was very nervous. But he had a plan. He would divide his group into two parts. That way, if Esav attacked one group,

the second group would run away. He prayed to God and asked for His protection.

The next day, Jacob sent cattle, sheep, goats, camels, and donkeys as presents for his brother Esav. He hoped the presents would make his brother feel less angry with him. Then he took his wives and his children across the nearby Yabbok river, just in case Esav decided to attack.

That night, Jacob remembered that he had left some jars on the other side of the river, and he went back for them, all alone.

As he was collecting the jars, someone suddenly grabbed him. Jacob couldn't see who it was, but the man was strong, so strong that he managed to pull one of Jacob's thigh muscles. But Jacob didn't give up. He fought with the stranger through the night.

As the first rays of the sun broke through the clouds, the person Jacob was fighting said, "Let me go. I am an angel, the guardian angel of Esav, and I must pray to God now."

"No, I will not let you go unless you bless me first," Jacob said.

"What is your name?" asked the angel.

"I am called Jacob," Jacob answered.

"From now on, you will not be called Jacob. Your new name will be Israel," the angel said. "For you have fought with an angel and with Lavan and Esav, and you have won."

Jacob let the angel go. But as he began to walk back to his family, his thigh hurt him, and he limped. That's why, until this day, Jews do not eat the part of the animal called Jacob's sinew, in memory of the great battle between the angel of Esav and Jacob. And from then on, the Hebrews were called *Israelites*, or *The Children of Israel.*

Jacob reached his family just as his brother Esav arrived. Esav ran to greet him, and they hugged each other, and cried.

Jacob's plan had worked. Esav, happy with his presents, left without harming him.

Shimon And Levi And The People Of Shechem

On their way home, Jacob and his group stopped in the city of Shechem, which was in Canaan.

One day, Deena, Jacob's daughter, was walking through the marketplace, looking at interesting items for sale. The prince of the city, who was also named Shechem, saw her, and wanted to marry her. He convinced her to come to his palace, but then he wouldn't let her go.

Shechem begged his father, King Hamor, to ask Jacob to let him marry Deena. King Hamor took his son and came to Jacob's tent. "If you will let Shechem marry your daughter, Deena," the king said, as they sat down, "we will let your sons marry our daughters, and in this way you will be part of our nation."

Jacob was very upset and didn't know what to do. But Shimon and Levi, two of his sons, had a plan. They said to Hamor, "We are forbidden to allow our women to marry anyone without a Brit Milah. Only if you and your people circumcise yourselves, will we agree to your suggestion." Shechem and Hamor accepted the brothers' condition and returned to the city.

"Hear me, people of Shechem," the king announced. "If we agree to circumcise ourselves, then we will be able to marry their daughters, and take everything they have. Their cattle and their property will be ours, if we do this."

Since Jacob was very rich, this sounded like a good idea to the people. They agreed to make a Brit Milah on all of their males. But after the circumcision, they were very weak. On the third day, when they were weakest of all, Shimon and Levi — without asking permission from their father — rescued Deena by silently entering the city and killing all the men.

When they returned, Jacob was very upset. He didn't agree with what they had done. He was sure that his sons would just rescue Deena while the people of Shechem were weak.

"Now others will come to kill us for killing the people of Shechem. Many nations will take up the sword against us," Jacob warned his children.

But God protected Jacob. All the nations in the area became afraid of Jacob and his family.

Not long after, Rachel gave birth to Jacob's youngest son, Benjamin. Then she died, and was buried on the way to Bet Lechem.

The Children Of Israel

Jacob had twelve sons. *Reuven, Shimon, Levi, Judah, Issachar,* and *Zebulun* were Leah's sons. *Joseph* and *Benjamin* were Rachel's sons. *Dan* and *Naftali* were Bilhah's, Rachel's maidservant's sons. *Gad* and *Asher* were Zilpah's, Leah's maidservant's sons.

The Coat Of Many Colors
וישב

Jacob reached the land of Canaan, where he settled with his family. Of course, he loved all his children, but one child in particular was his favorite: Joseph.

To show his love, Jacob gave Joseph a dazzling coat of many colors, which Joseph wore all the time. The other brothers were very jealous.

But things might have worked themselves out, had Joseph not started talking about his dreams.

"We were all in the field together," Joseph told his brothers, "binding our straw into bundles. Suddenly, my bundle stood straight up and your bundles came over and bowed down to my bundle!"

"What?!" exclaimed Joseph's brothers. "Do you think that you, our little brother, will be king over us? Do you think we will bow down to you?!" And the brothers got up and left in a huff.

Instead of keeping quiet, Joseph called everyone together again, to tell them his latest dream.

"In this dream, the sun, the moon and eleven stars all bowed down to me!"

"What nerve," said one of the eleven brothers. "Now you want to tell us that our father, mother, and all of us will bow down to you? What *chutzpah!*"

Even Jacob was upset. He could see how angry Joseph was making his brothers. "Don't be silly," he told Joseph in front of the others. "Why would all of us be bowing down to you? Stop talking nonsense." Jacob knew that sometimes dreams do come true, but he didn't want there to be any fights among the brothers.

One day, when Joseph was seventeen years old, his father called him, saying, "Joseph, your brothers are tending the sheep in Shechem. Go and find out how they are doing, and let me know."

Joseph went to Shechem, but his brothers had already left. He rushed to catch up to them.

Joseph's brothers saw his bright coat in the distance, and knew he was coming.

"Look, here comes the Dreamer," one of them remarked.

"He's probably come to tell us another one of his dreams. Let's get rid of him once and for all," a second brother said.

"Good idea," added a third brother. "Let's see what happens to his dreams then!"

Suddenly, the oldest brother, Reuven, got up and said, "No. Let's not lift our hands to hurt him. We can throw him into a pit. The snakes and scorpions will do the rest." But secretly, Reuven planned to come back and rescue his brother from the pit.

When Joseph reached his brothers, they grabbed him, ripped off his beautiful coat, and threw him into the pit.

Meanwhile, Reuven had to do some errands, but he warned the brothers not to harm Joseph while he was gone.

As the brothers were sitting down to eat, they saw a caravan of Arabs approaching. The camels were loaded with sweet spices and other valuable things.

"Why should we let Joseph die in the pit, when we can sell him to these traders?" Judah suggested to his brothers.

The brothers discussed this idea and decided to pull Joseph out of the pit. They brought him to the Arab caravan and sold him.

When Reuven returned, he found the pit empty. "Where is Joseph?" he demanded. The others told Reuven what they had done.

"What?" he shouted. "Don't you understand? This will kill our father!"

The brothers decided they would tell their father that a wild animal had killed Joseph. They killed a goat and dipped Joseph's coat into its blood, making sure to tear the coat in many places.

"Now, no one will know the truth," the brothers said, feeling certain they would get away with it.

When they went back home, they showed the bloody coat to Jacob.

"OH NO!" Jacob shouted, grabbing the coat. "What happened?"

"We found the coat, father," said Reuven. "He must have been killed by wild animals."

Jacob ripped his own clothes as a sign of mourning and cried. All of his children tried to comfort Jacob, but he wouldn't listen. He was heartbroken that his favorite son was gone.

The Wine Server And The Baker

The caravan continued on its way. When it reached Egypt, the traders sold Joseph to the captain of the king's guards, Potifar.

Potifar liked Joseph, and made him the head of his household. At first his wife also liked Joseph, but then she became angry when he wouldn't let her boss him around the way she liked. So, she told lies about him, and before he knew it, Joseph was thrown into jail.

While in jail, he met two of the king's servants, the wine server and the baker. The wine server had been thrown into jail because a fly had flown into the wine he was serving the king. The baker had accidently served the king bread with some pebbles in it.

One night the wine server and the baker each had a dream. They told Joseph their dreams.

"I dreamt that there was a vine with three branches," said the wine server, "and it was growing grapes. Then I made the grapes into wine, and poured it into King Pharaoh's cup."

"God has given me the ability to understand dreams," Joseph told the wine server, "and I think I know what your dream means." Joseph then told the wine server that in three days the king would give him back his job.

The baker liked that explanation. He was anxious to hear what good things Joseph would tell *him*.

"I dreamt that I had three baskets of white bread on my head," he said. "Then a bird came and ate some bread right out of the basket!"

Joseph was quiet for a moment. He didn't have good things to say to the baker. His dream meant something very sad.

"Well, what does it mean?" asked the impatient baker.

Joseph told him. "In three days Pharaoh will take you out of prison too, but you will not go back to your job. Pharaoh will kill you, for it is your fault that a stone was found in his bread."

Sure enough, three days later, it was Pharaoh's birthday, and he made a big party for everyone. He gave his wine server back his job, since it wasn't really his fault that a fly had flown into the wine. But he didn't forgive the baker, and hanged him for leaving a stone in his bread.

"Don't forget to tell the king who told you what your dream meant," Joseph reminded the wine server as he was leaving the jail.

"I most certainly will," the wine server assured him.

But, of course, he completely forgot about Joseph.

Pharaoh's Dreams　מקץ

Two years later, Pharaoh, the king of Egypt, woke up in the middle of the night, very troubled. He called for all his advisors and magicians to come at once.

"I have had two very disturbing dreams and I need someone to tell me what they mean," the king announced.

But no one could explain to Pharaoh what his dreams meant. Suddenly, the wine server remembered the Hebrew, Joseph, who had explained his dream.

"I know someone who can interpret your dream," he told the king. "Only, he's in jail right now."

The king was so disturbed by his dreams that he ordered his guards to bring Joseph to him. "I can always throw him back into jail if I don't like what he says," the king said.

When Joseph appeared, he told the king, "Your Excellency, please tell me your dreams. I will pray to my God to tell me what your dreams mean."

So Pharaoh told Joseph his dreams.

"I was standing at the river's edge, and I could see seven fat cows feeding on the grass. Suddenly, seven very scrawny, sick cows appeared and ate up the fat ones. After they ate the fat cows, the scrawny cows looked just as skinny and sickly as before!"

"Then I woke up from my dream. But I fell asleep again and had another dream," continued Pharaoh. "In this dream, I saw seven full ears of corn. And then seven dried out, thin ears of corn appeared, and swallowed up the full ones. After they ate the full ones, the thin ears of corn looked just as dried out as before!"

Pharaoh turned to Joseph. "I told these dreams to all of my advisors and magicians, and no one could explain them to me."

"Both dreams mean the same thing," Joseph told Pharaoh. "There will be seven years of plenty in Egypt. But then there will be seven years of famine, when nothing will grow."

"What should we do?" asked the king.

"Pharaoh should find a wise man and set him over the land of Egypt," Joseph advised. "This man will be in charge of storing food during the good years, so there will be enough left for the hard years."

Pharaoh heard Joseph's words and realized that he was right. "We will not find a man who is wiser than you are," Pharaoh said to Joseph. "You will be in charge of my house, and you will be second only to me."

Then Pharaoh gave Joseph beautiful clothes to wear, and a gold necklace, and put him in a royal chariot.

Soon after, Joseph married and had two sons, Menashe and Ephraim.

Joseph Meets His Brothers

Things had happened just as Joseph had said. First, there were seven years with lots of great harvests, when everything grew. The granaries were full. Then the famine started, and the earth was parched and dry. Nothing could grow.

But Joseph had stored away plenty of food during the good years. People came from everywhere to Egypt to buy food from Joseph.

In Canaan, Jacob and his family were hungry too. When Jacob heard that food was being sold in Egypt, he sent his sons there to buy grain. Only Benjamin, his youngest son, stayed home.

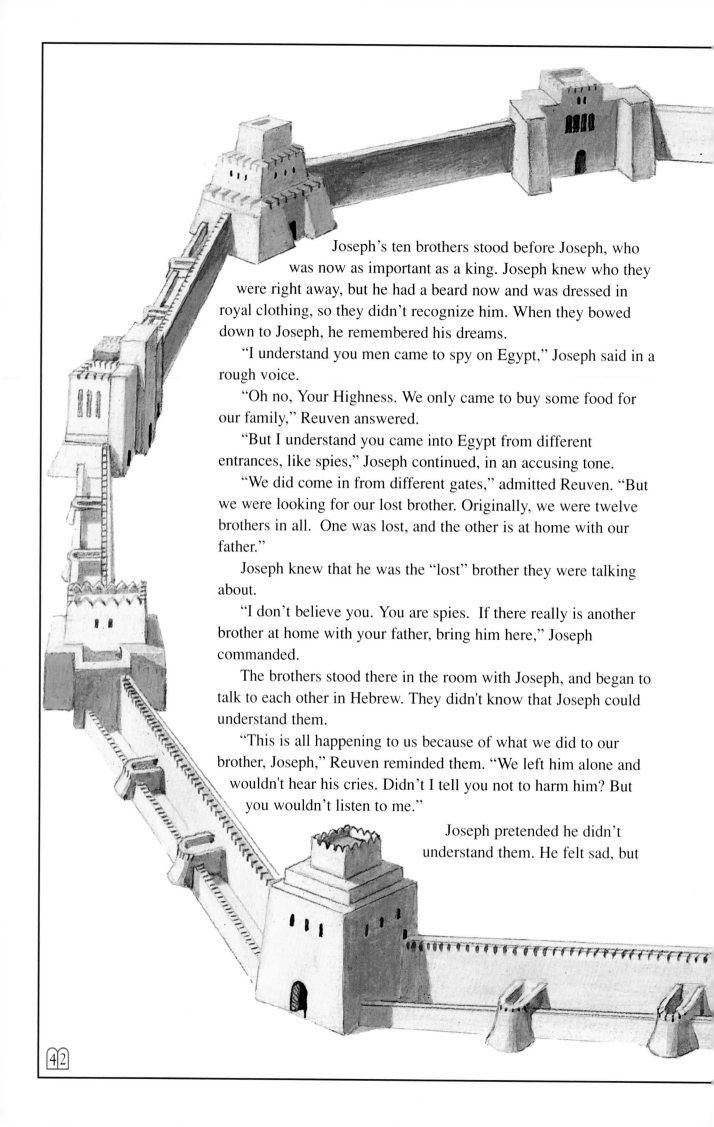

Joseph's ten brothers stood before Joseph, who was now as important as a king. Joseph knew who they were right away, but he had a beard now and was dressed in royal clothing, so they didn't recognize him. When they bowed down to Joseph, he remembered his dreams.

"I understand you men came to spy on Egypt," Joseph said in a rough voice.

"Oh no, Your Highness. We only came to buy some food for our family," Reuven answered.

"But I understand you came into Egypt from different entrances, like spies," Joseph continued, in an accusing tone.

"We did come in from different gates," admitted Reuven. "But we were looking for our lost brother. Originally, we were twelve brothers in all. One was lost, and the other is at home with our father."

Joseph knew that he was the "lost" brother they were talking about.

"I don't believe you. You are spies. If there really is another brother at home with your father, bring him here," Joseph commanded.

The brothers stood there in the room with Joseph, and began to talk to each other in Hebrew. They didn't know that Joseph could understand them.

"This is all happening to us because of what we did to our brother, Joseph," Reuven reminded them. "We left him alone and wouldn't hear his cries. Didn't I tell you not to harm him? But you wouldn't listen to me."

Joseph pretended he didn't understand them. He felt sad, but

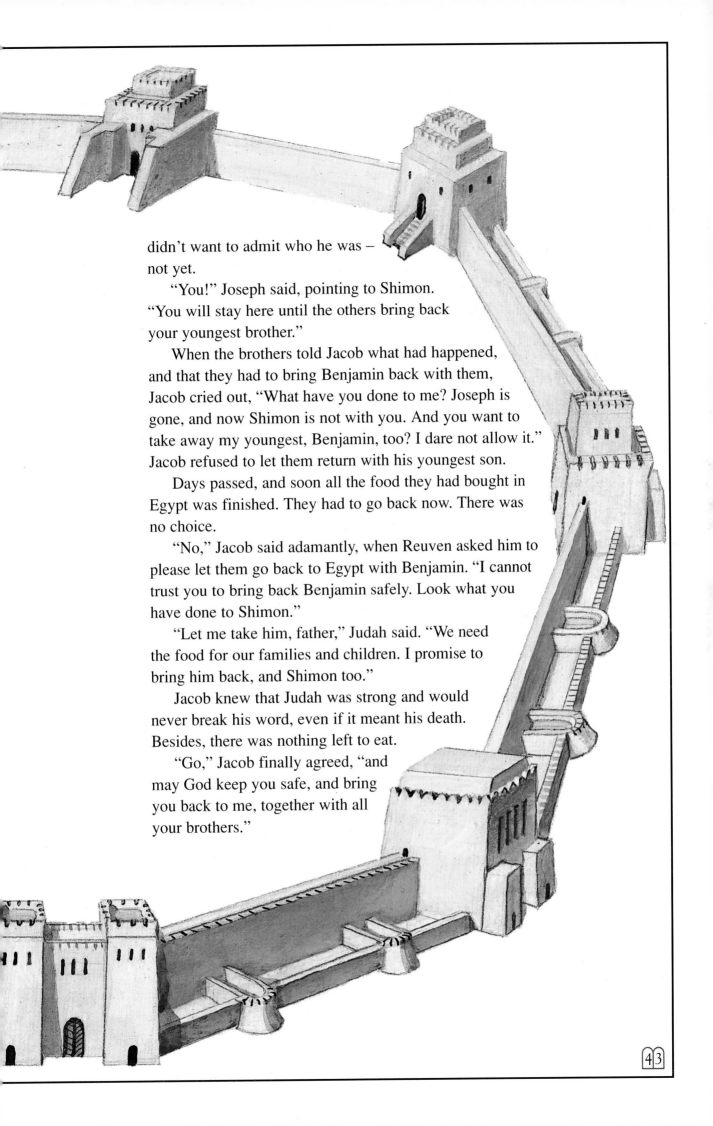

didn't want to admit who he was –
not yet.

"You!" Joseph said, pointing to Shimon.
"You will stay here until the others bring back
your youngest brother."

When the brothers told Jacob what had happened,
and that they had to bring Benjamin back with them,
Jacob cried out, "What have you done to me? Joseph is
gone, and now Shimon is not with you. And you want to
take away my youngest, Benjamin, too? I dare not allow it."
Jacob refused to let them return with his youngest son.

Days passed, and soon all the food they had bought in
Egypt was finished. They had to go back now. There was
no choice.

"No," Jacob said adamantly, when Reuven asked him to
please let them go back to Egypt with Benjamin. "I cannot
trust you to bring back Benjamin safely. Look what you
have done to Shimon."

"Let me take him, father," Judah said. "We need
the food for our families and children. I promise to
bring him back, and Shimon too."

Jacob knew that Judah was strong and would
never break his word, even if it meant his death.
Besides, there was nothing left to eat.

"Go," Jacob finally agreed, "and
may God keep you safe, and bring
you back to me, together with all
your brothers."

Joseph Reveals His True Identity   ויגש

The brothers were brought before Joseph as soon as they arrived.

When Joseph saw Benjamin, he was no longer angry at his brothers. "How is your father?" Joseph asked the brothers.

"Our father is well," they answered.

"And is this the younger brother you told me about?" he asked them.

"Yes," they answered.

"We've bought the food we need," Judah added, "and we would like to return home."

"You may go," Joseph told them.

When they left, Joseph told his servant, "Fill their bags with grain, and put each man's money back in his sack. Then put my silver cup in the sack of the youngest brother."

The next morning, the brothers left on their way home, but before they had travelled very far, Joseph sent some men to chase after them.

"Why have you paid back our kindness with evil?" one of the men demanded, when they caught up with the brothers. "The prince's silver cup is missing."

"We have done nothing," the brothers answered. "If you find the cup in our things, you can punish all of us," they announced, confidently.

So, Joseph's men began to search, starting with the oldest brother's things. And finally, in Benjamin's sack, they found Joseph's silver cup.

"What have you done?" Joseph demanded of them, back at the palace.

"What can we say?" Judah answered. "We will all become your servants now."

"No," answered Joseph. "Only the man who had the cup in his sack will become my servant. The rest of you can return to your father."

Joseph waited to see what his brothers would say. Would they leave Benjamin alone, just as they had left Joseph long ago?

Then Judah stepped forward. He had decided he would die rather than leave Benjamin in Egypt.

"Please do not be angry at me, Your Majesty. But if I go back to my father without our youngest brother, our father will surely die of sorrow. I beg of you, take me as your servant instead."

Joseph realized that Judah was willing to sacrifice his life for his brother. He saw how worried the others looked. The brothers had learned their lesson.

"Clear the room," he ordered. "Leave only these men here with me," he told his servants. Once everyone had left, Joseph could not control himself any longer. He began to cry. Then, for the first time in many years, he spoke in Hebrew.

"I am Joseph. Is my father still alive?"

The brothers were shocked! Could this be?! Was this really their brother, Joseph, after all these years? How had he become the prince of Egypt?

Their shock turned to embarrassment and fear. They remembered all too clearly what they had done.

"Please come near," Joseph coaxed. "Don't be afraid. I am not angry with you for what happened long ago. God sent me here, and put me in charge of Egypt, so that I could save you with the food I have stored."

Joseph went over and hugged his younger brother, Benjamin. He then sent everyone back to Canaan with wagonloads of gifts for his father, and food for the way home. When the brothers arrived home and told their father what had happened, Jacob could hardly believe it.

"I am so happy. My son Joseph is alive. I will go to see him now before I am too old to make the journey."

Shepherds Or Warriors

So, Jacob went down to Egypt with all of his children and their wives and families. He settled in Goshen, one of the most fertile areas of Egypt. Joseph wasted no time, and went to Goshen himself to meet his father.

"I am so happy that you are alive," Jacob told his son, Joseph, as they hugged each other.

"I missed you too," Joseph declared. "But we have a problem,

which I think I can solve. The king wants to put all my brothers into the army. This is considered a big honor in Egypt."

"But we are not warriors," Jacob said.

"I know that, father," Joseph continued. "My plan is to tell him that we are a family of shepherds. I will introduce the king to my weakest-looking brothers, and he will see that our family is not army material. This way, the king will give word that you are to be shepherds in Goshen, and that the Egyptians are to leave you in peace."

Joseph took his father and five of his weakest-looking brothers to the king.

"What do you do?" Pharaoh asked the brothers.

"We are all shepherds," they answered him. "We have come here to be with our brother Joseph, and to graze our flocks," they told the king.

The king saw that indeed they were not trained in the ways of soldiers and said, "Let your family live in the land of Goshen." But he still wanted to honor them, so he added, "And let them take care of my cattle too."

Then Pharaoh turned to Jacob. He saw the wrinkles on his face, and his long, white beard.

"How old are you?" Pharaoh asked Jacob.

"I am 130 years old," Jacob answered. "But they have been difficult years," he sighed, remembering his problems with Esav, Lavan, and the years of mourning for Joseph.

Then Jacob blessed the king, and returned with his sons, to Goshen.

Joseph Makes New Laws

Before long, the people of Egypt ran out of money, and they came crying to Joseph. "This famine is killing us. Give us food! We have nothing left to eat!"

Joseph spoke in the name of Pharaoh. "If you give us your

animals, we will give you bread." So, the people exchanged all of their horses, and donkeys, and cows, and sheep for bread. They were sure the famine would soon end.

But the next year, when their supplies ran out, the people returned to Joseph. "We have no more money, and no more animals to trade for food — only our land and ourselves. We will become slaves to Pharaoh if you will only give us something to eat, and seeds to plant, in order to grow more food."

Joseph took all of the people's lands for Pharaoh, and moved the people from city to city. In this way, they would know what it was like to be a newcomer to the land — like Joseph's family — and not mistreat the Hebrews.

Then, after he had given the people food and seed, Joseph announced, "Plant these seeds. But one fifth of everything that grows from them must be given over to Pharaoh."

The people readily agreed, because now they would have enough food to last through the famine. Pharaoh was delighted too, because now he owned all the land of Egypt. And Joseph was pleased, because his family would be safe.

Jacob Switches Hands   ויחי

Jacob lived the last seventeen years of his life in Egypt. When he was 147 years old, he called his son Joseph to his side, saying, "Promise me that you will bury me in the Cave of Machpelah, near my fathers, and not here in Egypt."

Joseph promised. Not long afterwards, he brought his two sons, Ephraim and Menashe, to his father for a blessing. Jacob told the two boys, "You will be counted just like my children, in everything." That's why later, when the Twelve Tribes of Israel are mentioned, Ephraim and Menashe are each counted as a tribe.

Ephraim, the younger boy, stood opposite Jacob's left hand, and Menashe, the older one, stood opposite Jacob's right hand. After all, it was the custom to give the older son the greater blessing with the right hand. But Jacob reached out his right hand, and put it on the younger son's head, and his left hand on the older one's head.

When Joseph saw this, he lifted up his father's right hand to switch it, but Jacob said, "I know what I am doing. The younger brother shall become greater than the older one. From him will come a great man (Joshua). But both will have many children. And, in the future, when the people bless their sons, they will say, 'May God make you like Ephraim and Menashe.' "

Then Jacob called the rest of his sons together, to bless them all before he died.

The Ways Of God

When Jacob died, Joseph went to speak to Pharaoh.

"I promised my father that I would take him to be buried in the land of Canaan. Please let me take him there, and I will come back as soon as I have carried out his wishes."

Pharaoh gave Joseph permission to carry out his promise. But after their father was buried, Joseph's brothers began to worry.

"Perhaps now that our father is gone, Joseph will hate us for what we did to him. Maybe he will punish us."

So, they went to Joseph, and asked him to forgive them. Joseph tried to explain how God had planned everything.

"Brothers, of course I forgive you," he told them. "For, while you meant me harm when you sold me, God turned that harm to good, and now we are all alive because of what you did. Do not fear, I will take care of all of you and your children."

And that's what he did.

When Joseph was 110 years old, he became ill and knew he was going to die.

"God will not forget you," he told his brothers. "He will bring you all out of Egypt, to the land that was promised to Abraham, Isaac, and Jacob.

"Only promise me that you will take my bones with you when you leave Egypt."

The brothers promised, and when Joseph died, the king buried him as a prince of Egypt.

From their small group of 70, the children of Israel multiplied and became many. They prospered, and lived in peace.

Until...

MIDRASHIM:
TALES OF OUR SAGES

In The Beginning

Why does the Torah tell us that God created light in the sky, and then, later, that God created the sun and the moon? Wasn't the light that God created, the sun and the moon?

Our rabbis suggest that the original light that God created was not the light we see today. It was a special light, much brighter than the light of our sun — over 60,000 times brighter! This light had the power to make people smarter than they could ever imagine. But God knew that the evil people in the world would benefit from this light, and that their ability to harm others would be multiplied as well. So God took this light and put it aside for the righteous people who will enjoy it in the next world. In its place, God left us much weaker lights — the sun and the moon that we see today.

The Garden Of Eden

Before Adam and Eve ate of the Tree of Knowledge they were clothed in a fingernail-like material that protected them from the elements and yet gave them complete freedom of movement. They lost this covering after they sinned.

On Saturday night, after the first stars come out, a special ceremony called *Havdallah*, "separation," is performed, which ushers out the Shabbat. During this ceremony the fingernails are held up to the Havdallah candle as a reminder of the nail-like clothing Adam and Eve wore in the Garden of Eden before they sinned.

Some say that Adam and Eve lost this special covering on Saturday night, and that is why it has become part of the Havdallah ceremony.

According to the Midrash, Adam was really the one who had told Eve it was forbidden to touch the Tree of Knowledge. She was only repeating what Adam had told her. For, when Adam heard the command not to eat from the tree, he decided to add to God's words, believing that by telling Eve not to touch the tree, his wife would not be tempted to eat the fruit. Naturally, when the snake pushed Eve into the tree and nothing happened, she began to doubt that anything Adam had said about the tree was true.

If only Adam had trusted his wife, and not added to God's words, what a difference it might have made!

God wanted the angels to see how smart Adam was.

"What would you name these animals?" God asked, as each animal passed before the angels.

"We don't know," the angels answered.

Then God brought all the animals to Adam. As each animal passed before him, Adam gave it a name that fit it perfectly! First, Adam named the animals in Hebrew, and then in all seventy other languages! He even knew the right name to give himself.

But, Adam realized that all the animals had a partner. He was the only one in the world without a partner. He was all alone. So, Adam asked God for a wife.

The Sages say that the Snake's punishment for convincing Eve to eat of the Tree of Knowledge, is strange. Why did he lose his legs?

The answer lies in the fact that before Adam and Eve ate of the Tree of Knowledge, they were able to roam freely between this world and the Heavens. They could go to what is today called, "the next world," by simply walking up toward the stars and beyond. Once they sinned, however, they lost this ability. They were grounded to this world. The only way to get to the next world, was to die.

For making Adam and Eve lose their ability to go up, to travel to the heavens, the snake lost his ability to stand up and walk as the other creatures do.

Noah And The Flood

Noah and his family worked very hard during the year that they were in the Ark. They hardly had a chance to sleep, because they were so busy feeding and taking care of thousands of animals and birds. There were some animals that got hungry in the morning, and others who had to be fed at night. On top of that, each type of animal ate a different kind of food. Some animals ate meat, some ate vegetables, and some ate worms!

But Noah's biggest problem was that some of the animals had short tempers, especially if they weren't fed on time. Once, Noah came late to feed the lion, and the lion got so angry, that he kicked Noah. Noah still limped when he left the ark.

The Tower Of Babel

The people who built the tower of Babel felt secure because they were one nation with one language and one purpose. They knew that God had promised Noah never to destroy the world again, and as one people, they felt God would not harm them.

So, as punishment for what they did, God divided the people into seventy groups and appointed a different angel to watch over each group. God alone watched over Abraham and his descendants.

The groups went on their way and soon became seventy different nations, each with its own language and customs. They soon understood that while God had promised Noah to never again destroy the whole world, a single nation — such as Sodom — could, and would be destroyed if it went against God's laws.

Abram And Lot

During Abram's time, there was a great war between five strong kings and four other powerful kings. The four kings destroyed the army of the five kings, and took many people captive, including the King of Sodom, and Lot, the nephew of Abram.

Abram had promised to protect Lot. So, when he heard what had happened, Abram asked those in his camp to come with him to rescue Lot, but they were afraid of the four kings. Only Eliezer, Abram's servant, agreed to go. Together, they attacked the army of the four kings, and, with God's help, destroyed their enemy.

Lot and the King of Sodom were rescued by Abram. The King was very grateful and offered many gifts to Abram. But Abram refused all the gifts.

"It is God who has saved you," Abram proclaimed. "I won't take a thread from you, not even a shoelace, so that you won't one day say, 'I, the King of Sodom, made Abram rich.' "

Because Abram refused to take even a thread from the king, God later rewarded Abram's children with the commandment of the threads called, *tzi-tzit*, which Jewish men wear on the corners of their clothing.

God Makes A Promise To Abraham

Abraham cared very much about people. He practiced *Chesed*, loving kindness. One of his greatest joys was being able to invite people into his tent and show them his hospitality. While most tents in the desert have only one door, Abraham's tent had four doors so that people could come in from all directions.

Abraham would run out to greet visitors and invite them into his tent. He would feed them and then ask them to thank God — not him — for the food. If the visitors had time, he and his wife, Sarah, would teach them about God. Soon, many people joined Abraham and his group, anxious to hear his message.

Two Terrible Cities

In Sodom, the people were mean and cruel. Some, like Lot's wife, Eeris, wouldn't even lend salt to their neighbors! And they loved to make strangers feel unwelcome.

One of their favorite tricks was to invite a stranger to sleep overnight in the town.

"But we only have one bed at the inn," they would say.

When the stranger came to the inn, he would find a very long bed.

"The rules in Sodom are," the people would tell him, "that you have to fit the bed, exactly."

"What does that mean?" the stranger would ask.

And then they would grab him and lie him down on the bed, and stretch him and stretch him until he fit the bed.

Lot had four daughters, and two of them were married to men of Sodom. When Lot was told that Sodom would be destroyed, he went to tell his daughters to leave.

"You must be kidding," the married daughters declared. "Everyone is having fun and we party throughout the night, and you want us to leave. Trust us, father, nothing is going to happen. And we certainly are not going anywhere."

Even Lot wasn't so sure he wanted to leave. He was very wealthy and he couldn't decide which of his treasures to take along. Finally, the angels grabbed him and his family and pulled them away from the city.

"Be happy you are being saved," they told him, "and forget your treasures. Whatever you do, don't look back!"

But Lot's wife felt badly about her two daughters who weren't coming! When she turned around to see if they had changed their minds, she was turned into a pillar of salt, the very salt she had refused to lend to her neighbors.

Abraham Passes The Test

While Abraham was on the mountain called Moriah, preparing to give Isaac back to God, a wicked angel appeared to Sarah and told her what was happening. Sarah didn't believe him, so she asked three giants, who lived nearby, to look as far as they could see, and tell her what they saw. They described Abraham and Isaac on top of the mountain, and how Isaac was tied up and Abraham was getting ready to sacrifice him.

Then Sarah knew the wicked angel had told her the truth and she was sure her son had gone to heaven. She became so sad, that her soul left her body, and she died. Everyone in Canaan missed Sarah because she had helped so many people.

Sarah was so great that God spoke directly to her. Even the angels listened to what she said. When King Solomon later wrote the song of *Ayshet Chayil*, A Woman of Valor, which many Jews sing today at the table on Friday night, he was thinking of Sarah, who was a righteous woman.

The Perfect Wife For Isaac

The midrash says that Rebeccah wondered why Eliezer didn't draw water from the well for himself.

"Perhaps he is too ill, with a contagious disease," she thought.

She wanted to offer him some water to drink, but didn't want to use the rest of the water in the jug after he had drunk from it. At the same time, she didn't want to embarrass Eliezer either, by pouring out the leftover water.

"I will give water to your camels too," she said, quickly pouring out the rest of the water after he had drunk, but before he could object and say that he had already given them water.

Some say that she made it seem as if the jug had slipped and the water spilled out. Then she refilled it and gave the camels some more.

Eliezer gave Rebeccah two gifts: a gold ring which weighed as much as half a shekel, and two bracelets, which weighed as much as ten gold shekels. Both of these were symbolic of things that would later be given to the Jewish nation.

The half shekel symbolized the half shekel to be given by every male from twenty years and above in the desert, when the census was taken. The two bracelets symbolized the two tablets of the Torah, and the ten shekels they weighed, represented the Ten Commandments which Rebeccah's children would receive at Mt. Sinai.

Twins

Rebeccah didn't know she was carrying two babies. But she knew something strange was going on. Whenever she passed near a House of Learning, she would feel one side of her pushing, as though trying to get out of her. That was Jacob, anxious to begin learning about God.

But, when she passed a house of idol worship, she would feel another side of her pushing, trying to get out. That was Esav, eager to begin his evil ways.

After they were born, both Jacob and Esav studied with their grandfather, Abraham, and their father, Isaac, until they were thirteen years old. Then their true natures began to develop.

Jacob spent most of his time learning about God, and Esav became a hunter. Jacob learned from his grandfather about helping others, while Esav spent his time catching animals and tricking people. He even tricked his father into thinking that he was kind and gentle. He served his father food and drink, so that Isaac would think he was a good son. But his mother, Rebeccah knew the truth about Esav. That's why she helped Jacob get the blessings of the firstborn from Isaac.

Jacob Takes The Blessings

Jacob ran away from his wicked brother, Esav. But Esav sent his son, Eliphaz, to chase after Jacob and kill him. He told his son that once Jacob was dead, they would get back the blessings of the first born.

Eliphaz didn't want to kill his uncle. He had grown up in Isaac's house, and learned it was wrong to kill. But Eliphaz didn't want to disobey his father, either. So, he took away Jacob's possessions, and all the gifts Jacob had planned to take to Lavan, Rebeccah's brother.

"Now I can tell my father that I killed Jacob. Because, after all," he convinced himself, "a poor man, without anything to his name, is just like a dead man."

Jacob's Ladder

On the way to Lavan's house, Jacob rested on Mt. Moriah, where he dreamed about the ladder and the angels.

As he was preparing to sleep, Jacob put a number of stones around his head, to keep the wild animals away. If a wild animal came near, he would hear it clopping on the stones.

Then Jacob went to sleep. While he slept, the stones around his head started arguing.

"*I* want to be under Jacob's head," said one of the stones.

"Why should *you* get the honor to have such a wonderful person resting on you?" asked another.

Finally, God solved the problem. He combined all the stones into one stone and put this stone under Jacob's head.

Lavan's Tricks

When Lavan heard that Jacob had come to visit, he quickly ran out to greet him. Lavan remembered that Eliezer, Abraham's servant, had come with camels loaded with treasures. Certainly, he thought, Abraham's grandson would come with much more!

When Lavan saw Jacob standing there alone, he hugged him, all the while patting Jacob's pockets to feel if he had jewels in them. Then he kissed Jacob on both cheeks, to check if he was hiding jewels in his mouth. Imagine his surprise when Jacob told him that he was running away from Esav and had nothing but the clothes on his back.

Lavan was so tricky, that when he wasn't trying to fool Jacob, he was busy fooling the townspeople. Before Jacob's wedding to Rachel (whom Lavan switched for Leah), Lavan called the townspeople together.

"You all know what I plan to do to Jacob. But if my nephew hears about it, he'll elope with Rachel and we'll never see them again. So, to be sure that all of you will keep quiet about my plan, I want each of you to bring me some security, a special food or drink. I'll hold onto it until the day after the wedding. If anyone says anything, then I'll keep the food or drink."

Sure enough, each one of the people brought something special — meat, wine, all kinds of delicious foods — which

Lavan used for the wedding celebration.

That's why the Torah tells us that Lavan gathered the people and then made a feast, instead of doing things the normal way, making a feast and then inviting the people. He gathered the townspeople so he could trick them into giving him the food for the wedding feast!

Jacob Begins The Journey Home

We can learn many things from the ways of our forefathers. For example, when Jacob went out to meet his brother Esav, he was very frightened. So, he prepared himself for the meeting with his brother in three ways:

First, he prayed to God, and told each of his sons to pray too.

Next, Jacob prepared many gifts for Esav. He sent his servants to his brother with herds of animals. But he told his servants to make sure there was plenty of space between the herds so it would look to Esav like there were lots of animals coming as gifts.

Finally, in case nothing else worked, Jacob prepared to fight. All his people had knives and swords hidden underneath their clothing. He separated the people into two groups too, so that if Esav would destroy one group, the other group could escape.

Jacob's three ways of defending himself have been used by the Jewish people throughout history, whenever an enemy has tried to destroy us.

First, we pray to God to give us peace and to let us get along with the nations around us.

Next, we sometimes have to offer gifts to our enemies so they will not hurt us. After all, no amount of money is worth a human life.

Lastly, we prepare to fight, and leave ourselves ways to escape so that we can save as many people as possible from the enemy.

Jacob Fights The Angel

Why did the guardian angel of Esav touch Jacob specifically on the thigh?

One midrash says it was the practice in those days to carry important papers tied to the hip. Esav's angel wanted to grab the contract Esav had given to Jacob when he sold his birthright for a bowl of red bean soup. The angel grabbed Jacob's hip in order to tear up the contract.

Another explanation suggests that the sons of Jacob failed to

honor their father when they let him go alone, in the dark, to get the jars that were left behind. They should have accompanied him and made sure he was safe. Because of their negligence, Jacob had to confront the angel of Esav without any help. He was touched on the thigh and limped, as a reminder to future Jewish generations of the importance of accompanying parents.

Shimon And Levi And The People Of Shechem

After leaving Lavan, Jacob heard that Esav was coming to meet him. Afraid of what Esav might do, Jacob hid Deena, his daughter, in a chest.

Our rabbis say that this was a grave error. He should have had more faith in God.

Jacob didn't want Esav to see his beautiful daughter. He might want to marry her. But a good wife can improve her husband. By marrying Esav, Deena would have made him a better man. She had the power to change Esav and could have been a good influence on him. Furthermore, Esav might have improved his ways just by seeing Deena, in order to prove to Jacob that he was worthy of being Deena's husband.

Jacob thought he was saving Deena from a terrible fate, but as the story of Shechem shows, she suffered an even worse fate.

The Coat Of Many Colors

Jacob loved Joseph very much. He was very old when Joseph was born. We learn from the story of Joseph that people should not love one of their children more than another. Joseph's brothers began to hate him and wanted to harm him because of his special coat, even though it wasn't really worth much money.

Joseph Interprets Dreams

The king's wine server and his baker plotted to kill the king. They put poison into his wine and his bread. But the king was saved because he found a fly in his wine and wouldn't drink it, and a pebble in his bread, and wouldn't eat it.

The king was angrier at the baker than at the wine server, because a fly could get into a cup at any time, even after it is poured, but a pebble is only left in the flour because of carelessness.

Joseph asked the wine server to remember him, and to try to

get him released too. The wine server wanted to remember his promise to Joseph, but because Joseph trusted in man instead of God, God made the wine server forget.

Pharaoh's Dreams

There were many steps leading up to Pharaoh's throne. Only very wise men, who knew seventy languages, could walk up all the steps and talk to Pharaoh, who sat at the top.

After Joseph explained Pharaoh's dream, the king wanted to make Joseph a nobleman. But Pharaoh's advisors didn't like that.

"He is only a poor, Hebrew slave," they said.

"But he doesn't look like a slave," Pharaoh declared. "He looks like a nobleman."

"Perhaps," the advisors said. "But noblemen can speak seventy languages, and this slave can hardly speak Egyptian!"

So, Pharaoh decided to test Joseph. He would not use a translator to speak to Joseph. If Joseph was indeed a nobleman, he would know the well-known Egyptian language.

That night, an angel came and taught Joseph all seventy languages. The next morning, Pharaoh called for Joseph and began to speak to him in Egyptian. When Joseph answered, Pharaoh let him climb up one step. Then, Pharaoh spoke another language, and Joseph answered in that language. Pharaoh let him go up another step.

Pharaoh continued speaking different languages and Joseph continued answering in the different languages, until, step-by-step he was almost at the throne where Pharaoh sat. There was only one step left between him and Pharaoh!

Then Joseph spoke to Pharaoh in Hebrew. But Pharaoh could not answer, because Pharaoh didn't know any Hebrew.

Pharaoh motioned Joseph to lean closer to him.

"You must promise me," he whispered, "that you will tell no one that you know more languages than I do."

"As you wish, great king," Joseph whispered back.

When the advisors saw that Joseph could speak seventy languages, they had to agree that Joseph was a nobleman.

Then, Pharaoh put Joseph in charge of all the people in Egypt. He was almost as important as Pharaoh himself.

Joseph Meets His Brothers

Joseph wanted to make sure he would find his brothers in case they came to Egypt to buy grain, so he made special rules:

    1. People couldn't send their servants to buy grain without at least one family member in attendance.

2. Each person could only buy one donkey-load of grain, and only at Joseph's store.
3. Everyone buying grain had to sign his name and write in the name of his father and grandfather.

Joseph read over the list of buyers and in this way discovered that his brothers had come to Egypt.

The brothers came into Egypt through ten different gates. Joseph accused them of doing this in order to spy out the country. But they told him they had entered through ten gates to avoid an *Ayin Harah*, the evil eye.

Joseph Reveals His True Identity

Although many years had passed, when the brothers came to Egypt, Joseph soon figured out who they were. After all, except for Benjamin, all the brothers had been older than him, and their beards, while longer or whiter than before, were no different. However, the brothers didn't recognize Joseph, because when they had last seen him he was only seventeen years old, and beardless!

When Joseph was ready to reveal his true identity, he sent all the Egyptians out of the room. He didn't want to embarrass his brothers in front of the Egyptians. Then, he turned to his brothers.

"You told me that your brother Joseph died. Are you sure?" Joseph asked.

"Yes, we are. He's dead" the brothers assured him.

Joseph became angry. "How can you lie?" he scolded them. "You sold him as a slave. I bought him, and can call him right now."

Joseph called out, "Joseph, son of Jacob, come here right now to speak to your brothers!"

Astonished, the brothers turned to see if Joseph was coming. When Joseph saw that his brothers were prepared to meet their brother, and ask his forgiveness, he said to them in Hebrew, "Who are you looking for? *I* am Joseph. Is my father still alive?"

The brothers turned back to Joseph with amazement, fear and awe in their eyes. They were so shocked that for a long time they could not speak a word! They hid their faces and wouldn't even look at Joseph.

Blessing The Sons Of Jacob

When Jacob felt he was dying, he called all his sons together. He wanted to tell them about the "end of days," when the Messiah would come. But God made it impossible for Jacob to give out this information.

Our Sages say that God doesn't want anyone to know when the Messiah will come. Knowing how long they would have to wait might make people give up on life, or, if they knew when the Messiah was coming, they might change their evil ways — just for that reason — and not because they really meant it.

Jacob wanted to hear his sons affirm their belief in God. When he asked them if they believed in the God of Abraham, Isaac, and Jacob, they answered with the words of *Shema*.

Shema Yisrael, Hear O Israel (Jacob's other name).
Hashem Elokaynu, Your God is our God.
Hashem Echad, God is One.

When Jews recite the Shema, they are also telling Israel — both Jacob and the Jewish people — that they are still keeping the faith, just as his sons did.

The Ways Of God

After Jacob died, Joseph asked Pharaoh for permission to bury his father in the land of Canaan. "I promised my father that I would take him back home."

"The wise men can take away your promise," Pharaoh answered Joseph.

"Then they will take away my other promise too," Joseph said. "Do you remember that I promised never to tell anyone that I speak more languages than you do?" Pharaoh had nothing to say to this. He decided to let Joseph go with his family to the land of Canaan. Joseph put Jacob's body into a beautiful golden coffin. Then he hung his crown on the coffin. Many Egyptians followed the brothers as they carried Jacob to his homeland. When they got there, Ishmael and Esav, and the kings of Canaan wanted to go to war against the brothers. But then they saw the big group that was carrying Jacob, and the Egyptians that were mourning for Jacob. Afraid, the kings of Canaan hung their crowns on Jacob's coffin too.